Henry and Eliza

Henry and Eliza

This edition of a story Jane Austen probably wrote at the age of 12, 13, or 14 has been produced as a group project by five tenth-grade students from The Brearley School in New York City, under the general editorship of Karen L. Hartnick, with Rachel M. Brownstein as consultant and contributing editor.

Preface: RACHEL M. BROWNSTEIN
Introduction: KAREN L. HARTNICK
Explanatory Notes: CATHERINE GOWL,
MAGGIE HARTNICK, ANN KELLY,
CASSIE MARLANTES, AND
KAREN L. HARTNICK
Illustrations: SARAH WAGNER-M^cCOY
Afterword: ANN KELLY
Book Design: WINSTON PEI
General Editor for the Juvenilia Press:
JULIET M^cMASTER

Juvenilia
PRESS

Edmonton, 1996

Henry and Eliza
ISBN: 0-9698271-7-2

Contents of the present edition,
including text, editorial matter, notes and illustrations:
Copyright © 1996 by Juliet McMaster
General Editor, Juvenilia Press
Department of English
University of Alberta
Edmonton, Alberta, Canada T6G 2E5

Cover Drawing: Sarah Wagner-McCoy
Formatting: Astrid Blodgett
Cover and Interior Design: Winston Pei/Black Riders Design

CONTENTS

ACKNOWLEDGEMENTS

The editors are grateful to Oxford University Press for their permission to use as their copy text the version of *Henry and Eliza* that appears in:

Volume VI, *Minor Works,* Chapman's edition of *The Works of Jane Austen,* as revised by B.C. Southam, Oxford University Press, reprinted 1987.

By permission of Oxford University Press

Thanks are also due to the Bodleian Library, University of Oxford, where Jane Austen's original manuscript of *Volume the First* is located (MS.Don.e.7), for permission to reproduce a page of the manuscript.

KAREN L. HARTNICK

PREFACE

Comparing them to prose that is generally considered more serious, Jane Austen praised novels for conveying to the world "the most thorough knowledge of human nature...in the best chosen language" (*NA*, 38). Admirers of Austen's own novels, who now take them very seriously, tirelessly debate her views about human nature, but give shorter shrift to her choices of language. This is not surprising: while it is easy to imagine Austen looking critically at the lexicon, or sneering at expressions like "the most amiable creature on earth," it is impossible to catch her in the crucial act of making sentences. Still, one can try. One can guess, for instance, at the pleasure it must have brought her to place the blunt word "cudgel" in the first sentence of *Henry and Eliza*—and conclude, perhaps, that she had even more fun coming up with that initial "As." More than her marriage plots, her minor characters, her modern understanding of materialism, or even her nice vocabulary, Austen's syntax conveys her distinctive voice, and her views.

As a girl she was already Jane Austen. The apparent clumsiness of characterization and plotting, in the early stories and sketches that she saved but never tried to publish, are clearly deliberate: one can tell from the sophisticated deployment of the words, the confident and elegant subordination, the careful parallelism and alliteration that lend a certain inevitability and even logic to the wackiest sequence of events. We are almost willing to believe the Dutchess of F would accept Eliza into her home on an innkeeper's say-so—willing, anyway, to savour the absurdity, and read on— when we learn of the lady that "her passions were strong, her freindships firm & her Enmities, unconquerable." Clearly, this writer is in charge.

Raised by the clause that begins a sentence, Austen's readers' expectations get satisfied by unsettlingly precise details: opening on a broad prospect, the first sentence ends by focusing narrowly on the heroine as an infant not more than 3 months old. Very soon Eliza is old enough to steal a banknote of £50, meet a duchess of about 45 and a half, be pursued by 300 armed men, spend a whopping £18,000 a year for three years, walk thirty miles without stopping, and along the way have two of her fingers bitten off by her two "rather hungry" children. While private jokes may be hidden in those particular numbers, every reader who has thought at all about the differences between fact and fiction can appreciate the formidable authority of the exact count.

The timing is what her admirers value most in Jane Austen's mature novels: the phrase that brings one up short, the sudden sharp focus on a detail to interrupt a discourse that has been lolloping along as if to take it for granted that narrator and characters and readers have more or less the same kinds of pleasant lives and expectations. Austen's timing will get better later, but in the juvenilia it is already good: the innocent prepositional or participial phrase is tucked into its sentence, in "Henry and Eliza," at precisely the place where it will explode to best effect. The familiar and the unexpected jostle one another, making the banal suddenly fresh; we get a new view of conventions and of ourselves, who are mired in convention without seeing it. A dish of cow-heel and onion is elegantly offered around a dinner table in Austen's juvenile playlet, "The Visit"; in *Henry and Eliza* the heroine, who began her adventures by stealing their money, decides to remedy her "unavoidable misfortunes" by returning "to her old freinds, Sir George & Lady Harcourt, whose generosity she had so often experienced & hoped to experience as often again." Conventional sentiments and conventional sentences are mocked at once.

Narrative time is pointedly put out of joint in many of these early stories: the more important of the events narrated do not take longer to read about, as they ordinarily do in fiction. Eliza's courtship and her marriage of several years, the births of her children and her husband's appearance and character, are briskly passed over, while a dramatic point is made of events devolving from the pause of a private family's carriage "to give the Postilion an opportunity of admiring the beauty of the prospect." Tellingly, the rules that govern class and gender are called in question here along with those that regulate narrative. In *Henry and Eliza*, as in *Mansfield Park*, all the trouble starts when the head of the household abandons his domestic responsibilities and goes off to seek a newer, profitable world.

One might argue that *Henry and Eliza* is a satire on the inferior, conventional fiction that young Jane Austen read and later improved on, or conclude that she jumbled the conventions for relating true histories of foundlings and fabulous romances, and for portraying ideal heroines and evil women, in order to make fun of both fashionable extremes. But such an argument, I think, would be wrong-headed. Literary conventions and constraints are invoked and foregrounded to make the point that they *produce* fiction, here—as they will be later, in Austen's longer and more "realistic" novels.

RACHEL M. BROWNSTEIN

A NOTE FROM THE ILLUSTRATOR

Though Jane Austen did not intend the characters in *Henry and Eliza* to be mice, her satirical writing style and goofy plot allowed me some creativity with the illustrations. The characters in the story are human and my decision to draw them as mice was based on my preferences (I have always loved drawing mice), rather than the text. Austen wrote the story for her younger brother, so that the work caters to a younger audience but appeals to audiences of all ages. I hope that my illustrations do the same.

SARAH WAGNER-M^CCOY

NOTE ON THE TEXT

The original source for *Henry and Eliza* is Jane Austen's manuscript of *Volume the First* (M.S. Don. e. 7) in the Bodleian Library of Oxford University. The first page of the manuscript of "Henry and Eliza," which is page 87 in the manuscript of *Volume the First*, is reproduced in this book.

Volume the First remained in the Austen family, through the descendents of Jane's youngest brother, Charles, until 1993, when it was acquired for the Bodleian Library. That same year R.W. Chapman was granted permission to publish *Volume the First*. The text was edited by Chapman and published by The Clarendon Press, Oxford, in 1933.

Our copy text of *Henry and Eliza* is the 1987 reprinting of R.W. Chapman's edition of Jane Austen's *Minor Works*, first published by Oxford University Press in 1954 and revised in 1969 by Brian Southam.

A page of Henry and Eliza, *reproduced by kind permission of the Bodleian Library, University of Oxford, from the manuscript of Jane Austen's* Volume the First, *MS.Don.e.7, p. 87.*

# INTRODUCTION

"No one who had ever seen Catherine Morland in her infancy, would have supposed her born to be an heroine," Jane Austen wrote in *Northanger Abbey*, the first of her novels to be offered for publication. Eliza, of *Henry and Eliza*, has in infancy all the makings of a heroine. Unlike Catherine, who was born "as plain as any" with a sallow skin and a mind "not less impropitious for heroism" (*NA*, 13), Eliza is a beautiful little girl at three months old. The "enchanting Graces of her face" and the precocity of her intellect signal that she *is* born to be an heroine.

Henry and Eliza, which is, like Fanny Burney's *Evelina*, a "History of a Young Lady's Entrance into the World," inverts the story of the traditional novel heroine. Rather than facing, as Elizabeth Elliot does in *Persuasion*, "the sameness and the elegance, the prosperity and the nothingness, of her scene of life" (*P*, 9), Eliza lives out the traditional male adventure—she leaves her family, travels, faces danger, demonstrates cunning and bravery, and defeats her enemies in armed battle. Marriage, central to the traditional heroine's story, is so unimportant in Eliza's that it is dismissed in a one-sentence letter to the Dutchess of F: "Madam we are married and gone." Eliza's husband's death is dismissed in a clause: "at the end of it Eliza became a widow without anything to support either her or her children." This "novel" ends not with the heroine's marriage, but with Eliza raising an army and demolishing a prison, for which she gains "the Blessing of thousands, and the Applause of her own Heart." Only in the juvenilia would Jane Austen allow her heroine a hero's rewards.

Jane Austen was the seventh of eight children born to Cassandra Austen and George Austen, Rector of Steventon. In the Rectory where Jane grew up there was "the flow of native wit, with all the fun and nonsense of a large and clever family."[1] The Austen chil-

dren, together with friends, neighbours and relations, often enter-
tained each other by reading aloud and by participating in amateur
theatricals. A penchant for writing ran in the family. Jane's mother
wrote amusing verses and her brothers James and Henry wrote ar-
ticles for *The Loiterer*, a weekly periodical they published during
their years at Oxford, mocking the literature of sensibility through
burlesque stories and letters. James wrote versified prologues and
epilogues to the family theatricals and other poetry, including an
elegy to Jane. Anna Austen, Jane's niece, tried her hand at writing
novels, which Jane critiqued; her nephew Edward wrote novels that
Jane called "strong, manly, spirited sketches, full of variety and
glow...."[2]

It is highly probable that Jane transcribed her childhood writings into three manuscript books in order to compile "a record of
her early work for the convenience of reading aloud to the family
and her close friends."[3] The original manuscripts of these stories no
longer exist, but the three volumes comprise a "collected edition of
the author's work up to June 1793,"[4] when Jane Austen was eight-
een. The transcriptions were made over a fifteen- to twenty-year
period.[5] The first eleven items are in childish handwriting and "on
stylistic evidence can be assigned to the earliest period of Jane
Austen's writing."[6] *Volume the First* includes the "novel" of *Henry
and Eliza,* which was most probably written somewhere between
1787 and 1789. From a family record, we learn that Jane remembered 1787, the year she was twelve, as the year she began "to
devote her spare time to writing."[7] *Henry and Eliza* is certainly one
of the stories from this early period.

Possibly it was written to amuse Jane's youngest brother,
Charles, who was four years her junior. In a letter to Cassandra,
Jane playfully referred to Charles as "our own particular little
brother" (parodying a description in Fanny Burney's *Camilla*).[8]
Inside the front cover of *Volume the First* Jane wrote, "For my
Brother Charles," and Cassandra wrote on a scrap of paper pasted
below: "For my Brother Charles/I think we can recollect that a few
of the trifles in this Vol. were written expressly for his amusement."[9]
If *Henry and Eliza* was one of these "trifles" this might explain its
fairytale elements: Eliza's abandonment as an infant, and her dis-
covery of her true parents in the denouement.

The character of Eliza was most likely inspired by Jane Austen's
cousin Eliza de Feuillide, née Hancock (1761-1813). She was a

frequent visitor at Steventon in the 1780's. In a visit to the Austens in December 1787, she took the star parts in the family theatricals performed in the Rectory barn.[10] Eliza's personality seemed as outrageous to her friends and family as the fictional Eliza's temperament does to the reader. Philadelphia Walter, her cousin and Jane's, writes of the "dissipated life she was brought up to."[11] As it turned out, Jane's story was prophetic of elements of her cousin's biography. There are uncanny parallels between the historical and the fictional Elizas—both had unusual birth stories and romantic interludes in France, both were flirtatious flaunters of convention, both were widowed at an early age and left with young sons to take care of, and both married men named Henry. While Jane's cousin didn't marry her Henry until years after the composition of *Henry and Eliza*, Jane probably observed her interest in Henry Austen during her visits to Steventon. Eliza, then married to a Frenchman, visited Henry when he was at Oxford and wrote to her cousin Philadelphia, "I do not think you would know Henry with his hair powdered and dressed in a very *tonish* style," and added, "besides he is at present taller than his father."[12] In 1789, Eliza again wrote to her cousin, "I suppose you have had frequent accounts from Steventon, and that they have informed you of their theatrical performances, *The Sultan and Highlife* below-stairs. Miss Cooper performed the part of Roxalana and Henry the *Sultan*. I hear that Henry is taller than ever."[13] Clearly, Henry was on the mind of his married cousin, who was ten years older than he.

The real Eliza, the daughter of Mr. Austen's sister, Philadelphia, was born in India in 1761, but for many years lived with her mother in England. When she was seventeen (and Jane was three), Eliza's mother took her to Brussels and Paris to complete her education. Writing back to England from Paris, Eliza exclaims, "Indeed I am almost ashamed to say what a racketing life I have led,"[14] and later from London, "As to me I have been for some time past the greatest rake imaginable and really wonder how such a meagre creature as I am can support so much fatigue...."[15] The scandalous heroine of *Henry and Eliza* shares with Eliza de Feuillide a personality brimming with vitality, at once shrewd, self-confident and self-serving, flirtatious, determined and outrageously unrestrained. "I always find," wrote Eliza de Feuillide, sounding very like Eliza Cecil, "that the most effective mode of getting rid of temptation is to give in to it."[16] Eliza Hancock's first husband, a Captain in the

French army who called himself the Comte de Feuillide, was guillotined in 1794 during the Reign of Terror. The two had a son, Hastings, who died in childhood. Eliza married Jane's "favourite brother" Henry in 1797.[17]

Another of Jane's cousins figures in the mock dedication of this story. Mimicking the convention of novels of the day, *Henry and Eliza* is "humbly dedicated to Miss Cooper by her obedient Humble servant the author." Miss Cooper (also a Jane) was Jane Austen's first cousin, the daughter of her mother's sister. Jane and her older sister Cassandra had attended schools in Oxford, Southampton, and Reading with their cousin Jane Cooper, and she often visited Steventon and took part in family theatricals.

Jane Austen calls this story a novel, and in the eighteenth century the term "novel" was used to describe a variety of literary forms, including novellas and collections of fictional letters. There was, however, a consensus among critics "as to some of the qualities that should distinguish this mode of writing. It should be instructive, though preferably not blatantly so, it should have 'invention,'—a variety of interesting incidents and well supported characters; it should above all be probable, for probability distinguishes a novel from a romance, and its appeal to the reader's sympathies, and the consequent efficacy of its moral lesson, depend on probability."[18] Jane Austen burlesques all the conventions of the form in *Henry and Eliza*. Her story is highly improbable and morally outrageous, and most of the characters are barely described. For example, of the "hero," Henry Cecil, we learn nothing except that he abandons Lady Harriet to elope with Eliza, flees to France, and dies.

The author of *Henry and Eliza* ridicules, by absurd exaggeration, characteristics of sentimental romanticism. The melodramatic succession of calamities is conventional, but the mishaps themselves are bizarre and the tone unconventionally cavalier. By her offhand tone, Jane Austen downplayed the sensational elements of romantic fiction. She also poked fun at the convention of interpolating poems and songs, such as Eliza's song proclaiming her "Innocent Heart," sung after she robs her parents of a £50 banknote. In *Northanger Abbey*, Catherine reads "all such works as heroines must read to supply their memories with those quotations which are so serviceable and so soothing in the vicissitudes of their eventful lives" (*NA*, 15). Burlesqued also is the birth mystery plot, which Jane

Austen would ridicule again in *Northanger Abbey*. "There was not one family among their acquaintance," she writes there of Catherine Morland's family, "who had reared and supported a boy accidentally found at their door—not one young man whose origin was unknown" (*NA*, 16).

Burlesquing popular sentimental fiction was as familiar to Jane Austen as the novels she mocked. One of the books she enjoyed was Charlotte Lennox's *The Female Quixote* (published in 1752) which parodied French romances, credulous readers, and girls who sought to be heroines.

The theme of the proper relationship between parents and children, fundamental to the novels of Richardson and burlesqued in Restoration comedy, dominates *Henry and Eliza*, which was written by a child familiar with Richardson's novels and facing these issues herself. The childhood tale engages humorously in the discussion, while making fun of sermonizing novelists. Eliza uses moralistic language to justify her most outrageous breaches of filial piety, proclaiming that she will never swerve from "virtue's dear boundaries." In *Love and Freindship*, included in *Volume the Second* of the juvenilia and dedicated to "Madame la Comtesse de Feuillide," Jane returns to this theme, as Augustus and Sophia nobly disentangle themselves from the "shackles of Parental Authority, by a Clandestine Marriage"[19] and Augustus gracefully purloins a considerable sum of money from the desk of his unworthy father. In *Northanger Abbey*, which also concerns itself with moralizing and fiction, the narrator concludes by addressing the reader: "I leave it to be settled by whomsoever it may concern, whether the tendency of this work be altogether to recommend parental tyranny, or reward filial disobedience" (*NA*, 252). In the mature novels, the wit remains intrinsic to the style, but the underside of humour can be deeply serious.

Similarly, the social criticism which lies behind the caricatures of Lord and Lady Harcourt, representatives of England's ruling class, will surface in a more serious vein in the person of Sir Thomas Bertram in *Mansfield Park*, whose self-contradictions bring havoc to his family.

In the juvenilia laughter prevails. The words Virginia Woolf used in commenting upon *Love and Freindship* could be said of *Henry and Eliza* as well. "What is this note which never merges in the rest, which sounds distinctly and penetratingly all through the volume? It is the sound of laughter. The girl of fifteen [or thereabouts] is laughing, in her corner, at the world."[20]

KAREN L. HARTNICK

NOTES TO THE INTRODUCTION

1   Anna Lefroy, Jane Austen's niece, as quoted in *Jane Austen: Her Life and Letters, a Family Record* by R.A. Austen-Leigh and W. Austen-Leigh, p. 15. Mrs. Lefroy (1793-1872) was the daughter of Jane Austen's brother James. She married Rev. Benjamin Lefroy, Rector of Ashe. Her full name was Jane Anna Elizabeth Austen Lefroy, but she was known as "Anna."

2   To James Edward Austen, Dec. 16, 1816, *Jane Austen's Letters*, ed. Deirdre Le Faye, p. 323.

3   Preface by Brian Southam, *Jane Austen's Volume the First*, ed. R.W. Chapman, p.xv.

4   Preface by R.W. Chapman, *Jane Austen's Volume the First*, ed. R.W. Chapman, p. xviii.

5   Brian Southam, "The Juvenilia" (prefatory essay). *The Works of Jane Austen*, vol. VI, *Minor Works*, ed. Chapman, p. 1.

6   *Ibid.*, p. 2.

7   Austen, Caroline Mary Craven, *My Aunt Jane Austen* (Jane Austen Society, 1952), as quoted in *Jane Austen: A Family Record*, W. and R.A. Austen-Leigh and Deirdre Le Faye, p. 63.

8   *Jane Austen's Letters*, ed. Le Faye, p. 38. One piece of evidence we have that Jane Austen read and parodied Fanny Burney's *Camilla* is this parodic rephrasing of the passage in that novel (Vol. III, Bk. VI, Ch. X, p. 197 of 1802 ed.), in which the heroine is described as "my own particular niece."

9   Preface by R.W. Chapman, Jane Austen's *Volume the First*, p. xvii.

10 Much of the information in this passage is based upon an explanatory note in *Jane Austen: Catharine and Other Writings*, ed. Margaret Anne Doody and Douglas Murray, p. 298.

11 Philadelphia Walter to James Walter, September 19, 1787, *Austen Papers 1704-1856*, p. 123.

12 Eliza de Feuillide to Philadelphia Walter, August 22, 1788, *Austen Papers 1704-1856*, p. 133.

13 Eliza de Feuillide to Philadelphia Walter, February 11, 1789, *Austen Papers 1704-1856*, p. 138.

14 Eliza de Feuillide to Philadelphia Walter, March 27, 1782, *Austen Papers 1704-1856*, p. 102.

15 Eliza de Feuillide to Philadelphia Walter, April 9, 1787, *Austen Papers 1704-1856*, p. 123.

16 Eliza de Feuillide to Philadelphia Walter, quoted by Park Honan, *Jane Austen: Her Life*, p. 56.

17 W. and R.A. Austen-Leigh, in *Jane Austen: Her Life and Letters*, refer to him as "Jane's favourite brother, Henry," p. 4.

18 J.M.S. Tompkins, *The Popular Novel in England 1770-1800*, p. 19.

19 Jane Austen, *Love and Freindship, Minor Works*, ed. Chapman, p. 87.

20 Virginia Woolf, *The Common Reader*, p. 194.

*Sir George and Lady Harcourt...perceived...a beautiful
little girl not more than 3 months old.*

Henry[1] and Eliza[2]

a novel
Is humbly dedicated to Miss Cooper[3] by her obedient
Humble Servant

THE AUTHOR

As Sir George and Lady Harcourt were superintending the Labours[4] of their Haymakers,[5] rewarding the industry of some by smiles of approbation, & punishing the idleness of others, by a cudgel, they perceived lying closely concealed beneath the thick foliage of a Haycock,[6] a beautifull[7] little Girl not more than 3 months old.

Touched with the enchanting Graces of her face & delighted with the infantine tho' sprightly[8] answers she returned to their many questions, they resolved to take her home &, having no Children of their own, to educate her with care & cost.[9]

Being good People themselves, their first & principal care was to incite in her a Love of Virtue & a Hatred of Vice,[10] in which they so well succeeded (Eliza having a natural turn that way herself) that when she grew up, she was the delight of all who knew her.

Beloved by Lady Harcourt, adored by Sir George & admired by all the World,[11] she lived in a continued

Eliza...happy in the conscious knowledge of her own Excellence, amused herself, as she sate beneath a tree...singing.

course of uninterrupted Happiness, till she had attained her eighteenth year, when happening one day to be detected in stealing a banknote of 50£,[12] she was turned out of doors by her inhuman Benefactors.[13] Such a transition to one who did not possess so noble & exalted a mind as Eliza, would have been Death, but she, happy in the conscious knowledge of her own Excellence, amused herself, as she sate beneath a tree[14] with making & singing the following Lines.

SONG[15]

Though misfortunes my footsteps may ever attend
    I hope I shall never have need of a Freind
as an innocent Heart I will ever preserve
        and will never from Virtue's dear boundaries swerve.

Having amused herself some hours, with this song & her own pleasing reflections, she arose & took the road to M.[16] a small market town of which place her most intimate freind[17] kept the red Lion.[18]

To this freind she immediately went, to whom having recounted her late misfortune, she communicated her wish of getting into some family in the capacity of Humble Companion.[19]

Mrs Willson,[20] who was the most amiable creature on earth, was no sooner acquainted with her Desire, than she sate down in the Bar[21] & wrote the following Letter[22] to the Dutchess of F, the woman whom of all others, she most Esteemed.

"To the Dutchess of F."

Receive into your Family, at my request a young woman of unexceptionable Character, who is so good as to choose your Society in preference to going to Service.[23] Hasten, & take her from the arms of your
SARAH WILSON."

The Dutchess, whose freindship for Mrs. Wilson would have carried her any lengths, was overjoyed at such an opportunity of obliging her &[24] accordingly sate out[25] immediately on the receipt of her letter for the red Lion, which she reached the same Evening. The Dutchess of F. was about 45 & a half;[26] Her passions were strong, her freindships firm & her Enmities, unconquerable.[27] She was a widow & had only one Daughter who was on the point of marriage with a young Man of considerable fortune.[28]

The Dutchess no sooner beheld our Heroine than throwing her arms around her neck, she declared herself

*The Dutchess no sooner beheld our Heroine than...
she declared herself...much pleased with her.*

so much pleased with her, that she was resolved they
never more should part. Eliza was delighted with such a
protestation of freindship, & after taking a most affect-
ing leave of her dear Mrs Wilson, accompanied her grace
the next morning to her seat in Surry.[29]

    With every expression of regard did the Dutchess
introduce her to Lady Hariet, who was so much pleased
with her appearance that she besought her, to consider
her as her Sister, which Eliza with the greatest Condescension[30] promised to do.

    Mr Cecil, the Lover of Lady Harriet, being often
with the family was often with Eliza. A mutual Love

Mr. Cecil [and Eliza]...were united by the enamoured Chaplain.

took place & Cecil having declared his first, prevailed
on Eliza to consent to a private union,[31] which was easy
to be effected, as the dutchess's chaplain[32] being very
much in love with Eliza himself, would they were
certain do anything to oblige her.

The Dutchess & Lady Harriet being engaged one
evening to an assembly,[33] they took the opportunity of their
absence & were united by the enamoured Chaplain.

When the Ladies returned, their amazement was
great at finding instead of Eliza the following Note.

"MADAM
    We are married & gone.
                HENRY & ELIZA CECIL."

      Her Grace as soon as she had read the letter, which sufficiently explained the whole affair, flew into the most violent passion & after having spent an agreable half hour, in calling them by all the shocking Names her rage could suggest to her, sent out after them 300 armed Men,[34] with orders not to return without their Bodies, dead or alive; intending that if they should be brought to her in the latter condition to have them put to Death in some torturelike manner,[35] after a few years Confinement.

*Her Grace as soon as she had read the letter...
flew into the most violent passion.*

*In France they remained 3 years, during which
time they became the parents of two Boys.*

In the mean time Cecil & Eliza continued their
flight to the Continent,[36] which they judged to be more
secure than their native Land, from the dreadfull effects
of the Dutchess's vengeance, which they had so much
reason to apprehend.

In France they remained 3 years, during which
time they became the parents of two Boys, & at the end
of it Eliza became a widow without any thing to support
either her or her Children. They had lived since their
Marriage at the rate of 18,000£[37] a year, of which Mr
Cecil's estate being rather less than the twentieth part,[38]
they had been able to save but a trifle, having lived to
the utmost extent of their Income.

Eliza, being perfectly conscious of the derange-
ment in their affairs, immediately on her Husband's death
set sail for England, in a man of War of 55 Guns,[39] which
they had built in their more prosperous Days. But no

sooner had she stepped on Shore at Dover, with a Child in each hand, than she was seized by the officers of the Dutchess, & conducted by them to a snug little Newgate[40] of their Lady's, which she had erected for the reception of her own private Prisoners.

No sooner had Eliza entered her Dungeon than the first thought which occurred to her, was how to get out of it again.

She went to the Door; but it was locked. She looked at the Window; but it was barred with iron; disappointed in both her expectations, she dispaired of effecting her Escape, when she fortunately perceived in a Corner of her Cell, a small saw & Ladder of ropes.

[Eliza] fortunately perceived in a corner of her cell, a small saw and a Ladder of ropes.

[Eliza] determined to fling down all her Cloathes, of which she had a large Quantity, and then having given them strict charge not to hurt themselves, threw her Children after them.

With the saw she instantly went to work & in a few weeks had displaced every Bar but one to which she fastened the Ladder.

A difficulty then occurred which for some time, she knew not how to obviate. Her Children were too small to get down the Ladder by themselves, nor would it be possible for her to take them in her arms, when *she* did. At last she determined to fling down all her Cloathes, of which she had a large Quantity, & then having given them strict Charge not to hurt themselves, threw her Children after them. She herself with ease discended by the Ladder, at the bottom of which she had the pleasure of finding her little boys in perfect Health & fast asleep.

Her wardrobe[41] she now saw a fatal necessity of selling, both for the preservation of her Children & herself. With tears in her eyes, she parted with these last reliques of her former Glory, & with the money she got for them, bought others more usefull, some playthings for Her Boys and a gold Watch for herself.

But scarcely was she provided with the above-mentioned necessaries, than she began to find herself rather hungry, & had reason to think, by their biting off two of her fingers,[42] that her Children were much in the same situation.

To remedy these unavoidable misfortunes, she determined to return to her old freinds, Sir George & Lady Harcourt, whose generosity she had so often experienced & hoped to experience as often again.

She had about 40 miles to travel before she could reach their hospitable Mansion, of which having walked 30 without stopping,[43] she found herself at the Entrance of a Town, where often in happier times, she had accompanied Sir George & Lady Harcourt to regale themselves with a cold collation[44] at one of the Inns.

The reflections that her adventures since the last time she had partaken of these happy *Junketings*,[45] afforded her, occupied her mind, for some time, as she sate on the steps at the door of a Gentleman's house. As soon as these reflections were ended, she arose & determined to take her station at the very inn, she remembered with so much delight, from the Company of which, as they went in & out, she hoped to receive some Charitable Gratuity.[46]

She had but just taken her post at the Innyard before a Carriage drove out of it, & on turning the Corner at which she was stationed, stopped to give the

Postilion[47] an opportunity of admiring the beauty of the prospect. Eliza then advanced to the carriage & was going to request their Charity, when on fixing her Eyes on the Lady, within it, she exclaimed,

"Lady Harcourt!"

To which the lady replied,

"Eliza!"

"Yes Madam it is the wretched Eliza herself."

Sir George, who was also in the Carriage, but too much amazed to speek, was proceeding to demand an explanation from Eliza of the Situation she was then in, when Lady Harcourt in transports of Joy, exclaimed.

"Sir George, Sir George, she is not only Eliza our adopted Daughter, but our real Child."

"Our real Child! What Lady Harcourt, do you mean? You know you never even was with child.[48] Explain yourself, I beseech you."

"You must remember Sir George, that when you sailed for America, you left me breeding."[49]

"I do, I do, go on dear Polly."[50]

"Four months after you were gone, I was delivered of this Girl, but dreading your just resentment at her not proving the Boy you wished, I took her to a Haycock & laid her down. A few weeks afterwards, you returned, & fortunately for me, made no enquiries on the subject. Satisfied within myself of the wellfare of my Child, I soon forgot I had one, insomuch that when, we shortly after found her in the very Haycock, I had placed her, I had no more idea of her being my own, than you had, & nothing I will venture to say would have recalled the circumstance to my remembrance, but my thus accidentally hearing her voice, which now strikes me as being the very counterpart of my own Child's."

"The rational & convincing Account you have given of the whole affair, said Sir George, leaves no doubt of her being our Daughter & as such I freely forgive the robbery she was guilty of."

A mutual Reconciliation then took place, & Eliza, ascending the Carriage with her two Children returned to that home from which she had been absent nearly four years.

No sooner was she reinstated in her accustomed power at Harcourt Hall, than she raised an Army,[51] with which she entirely demolished the Dutchess's Newgate, snug as it was, and by that act, gained the Blessings of thousands, & the Applause of her own Heart.[52]

FINIS

EXPLANATORY NOTES

1 **Henry:** In *The Popular Novel in England 1770-1800*, J.M.S. Tompkins observes that, "on a moderate estimate, eighty per cent. of the heroes are called Henry" (Tompkins, 57-58). Jane Austen herself liked the name Henry, as we discover in her ironic comments in a letter of October 14, 1813, to her sister Cassandra. A house guest is described as "5 or 6 & 20, not ill-looking and not agreable,—He is certainly no addition.... They say his name is Henry. A proof how unequally the gifts of Fortune are bestowed...." JA 's favourite brother was Henry Austen (1771-1850). "Leslie Castle," another of JA's juvenile pieces, was dedicated to Henry (*MW*, 110), and Henry later acted as his sister's literary agent.

2 **Eliza:** The name is probably associated with Eliza Hancock de Feuillide (1761-1813), JA's cousin, whose second marriage (December 31, 1797) was to be to Henry Austen.

3 **Miss Cooper:** JA dedicated the stories in the juvenilia to various members of her family. Jane Cooper (1771-1798) was the daughter of Mrs. Austen's sister Jane and the Reverend Edward Cooper, Rector of Whaddon, near Bath. "A Collection of Letters" in *Volume the Second* of the juvenilia is also dedicated to this cousin. Miss Cooper became Mrs. Williams on December 11, 1792, so we know that *Henry and Eliza* was written before then.

4 **Labours:** Young JA capitalizes several nouns at random during the course of the novel. Benjamin Franklin, an early contemporary of Austen's, capitalizes all of his nouns. Capitalization was not yet standardized.

5 **Haymakers:** People who make hay out of mown grass: people who lift, toss and spread the hay after it is mown (OED). At the end of her life, JA put a gentleman among his haymakers, rather than separating the aristocrat from the people as in *Henry and Eliza*. In *Sanditon*, her last novel, JA writes of "the Proprietor of the Place, who happened to be among his Haymakers at the time, and three or four of the ablest of them summoned to attend their master" (*Sanditon, Minor Works*, 365)

6 **Haycock:** A cone-shaped heap of hay in the field (OED). The term may be most familiar to modern American readers from the nursery rhyme character, Little Boy Blue, who was found "under a haycock

fast asleep." The first recording of "Little Boy Blue" was published between 1754 and 1768, in *The Famous Tommy Thumb's Little Story-Book.* The term "haycock" dates from the thirteenth century.

7   **beautifull:** This spelling of the word was common in the sixteenth and seventeenth centuries, and lingered into the eighteenth century. In the late eighteenth century, spelling had not been standardized; therefore the variants that appear in the text were acceptable, e.g., "agreable," "dreadful," "dispaired," "discend," "cloathes," and "speek." At this stage of her life JA was an inconsistent speller and several variants may appear in one piece. Brian Southam uses several spellings in *Volume the First* as a guide to dating the works therein. "Prominent among these is the suffix—*full*—in such compounds as beautifull, dreadfull, usefull, faithfull, & c....These spellings are general in the early pieces; in the later transcriptions, some of the words are spelled conventionally; and occasionally...she returned to the earlier pieces, normalizing the spelling in places...[which assists in judging the order of the transcriptions]...*beautifull* occurs in the earliest pieces, whereas in the last of the juvenilia...[in *Volume the First*] and in the other notebooks, Jane Austen prefers *beautiful.*" (B.C. Southam, *The Library*, p. 236).

8   **infantine tho' sprightly:** infant-like, although animated and cheerful. It is curious that "infantine" is opposed to "sprightly," as infants are often animated and cheerful. Perhaps JA was playing with words, alluding to the Latin word "infans" meaning "that cannot speak, without speech," in order to highlight the absurdity of baby Eliza's lively repartee.

9   **to educate her with care and cost:** Alliteration palliates catachresis. One can educate "with care," but usually it is "at cost." The cost of education was a concern to the Austen family, as Mr. Austen was often forced to take loans. Because of costs, the boys were not sent to boarding school. James and Henry were able to attend St. John's College, Oxford, as Founder's Kin of the Leighs, Mrs. Austen's family. This entitled them to pay no fees. Jane and Cassandra were taken out of the Abbey School at Reading, a boarding school for girls, because the tuition was prohibitive. Because of financial considerations, JA's third brother Edward was given in adoption to a wealthy, childless cousin of Mr. Austen, Thomas Knight, and his wife Catherine Knatchbull Knight. The Knights raised and educated Edward.

10   **Love of Virtue & a Hatred of Vice:** *Henry and Eliza* implicitly pokes fun at the Conduct Books and sermons for young women, written by Mrs. Chapone and others, on which eighteenth-century ladies were reared; Mr. Collins in *Pride and Prejudice* bores the Bennet sisters when he reads to them from Fordyce's *Sermons to Young Women* (1776).

11   **admired by all the World:** Like Richardson's *Clarissa*, Eliza is admired by many, but unlike Clarissa she suffers from narcissism and does not deserve to be admired. Unwarranted self-love is satirized in this early piece.

12 **50£:** There is a range of opinion on what the present market value of fifty pounds would be, in U.S. dollars, the lowest estimate found being $1,656 (Heldman, *Persuasions*, 12, 39). In any event, Eliza's is far more than a minor theft. The average per capita income in 1800 was 22£ (according to the librarian at the British Consulate in New York City). The Abbey School which Jane attended cost the Austens 35£ per annum.

13 **inhuman Benefactors:** The use of an oxymoron is satiric. Eliza, self-approvingly, steals from her benefactors; the narrative does not judge her but instead slips into her point of view.

14 **sate beneath a tree:** In the eighteenth century "sate" was often used as the past tense of "sit."

15 **Song:** Lines of poetry were meant to give emphasis to contemplative moments. It was a convention to intersperse them throughout the text; simultaneously setting them to music, however, is rare!

16 **M:** JA often uses initials instead of naming people or places in her stories. Brian Southam has observed that "in *Grandison* members of the aristocracy are referred to only by their initials. Hence Lord and Lady L. and Lord G. This was a convention of epistolary fiction: the letters were supposedly real and so the identity of these lords and ladies was to be respectfully concealed" (Southam, ed., *Jane Austen's 'Sir Charles Grandison,'* 118).

17 **freind:** Chapman states that "the spelling *freindship* is not eccentric. Boswell often wrote *freind*. And JA wrote *neice* and even *veiw*" (Chapman, *MW*, 2). Brian Southam observes that spellings in such words as "freind, beleif, greif, veiw," etc., and their formations are general in JA's early pieces and less general in her later work. "For example, at the beginning of the notebook JA writes fr*ei*nd, whereas at the other end, written in June 1793, she uses the more conventional spelling, fr*ie*nd...a form she was not employing in 1790" (Southam, *Library*, 236). It is little known that Austen corrected the original spelling of "freindship" in her story *Love and Freindship* on the title page of *Volume the Second* (*Library*, 233).

18 **red Lion:** The name of an inn. The sign outside an inn would depict the animal, bird, or other image which was its emblem. A White Hart Inn is mentioned in *The Watsons* and in *Persuasion*. In his edition of *The Minor Works*, Chapman includes a picture of the White Horse Inn at Dorking as an example of such an establishment.

19 **Humble Companion:** The only jobs that genteel women could take without a loss of caste were teacher, governess, or companion to a wealthy woman, for which they would earn a small salary along with room and board.

20 **Mrs. Willson:** The original transcription of *Henry and Eliza* read "Mrs. Jones" wherever Mrs. Willson is mentioned. Austen later crossed out "Jones" and substituted "Wilson" or "Willson."

21 **Bar:** Johnson defines this as "an enclosed place in a tavern or coffeehouse, where the housekeeper sits and receives reckonings."

Mrs. Wilson, the proprietor of the Red Lion Inn, uses this place to write her letter to the Dutchess of F.

22 **wrote the following letter:** Letters were used by novelists of the time to carry the plot, reveal character, or to make specific information stand out. JA continued to use letters (but not poetry) in her later work. *Love and Freindship* (completed in 1790), is an epistolary novel, as is *Lady Susan* (probably written in 1795).

23 **going to Service:** Eliza preferred becoming a companion to the Dutchess of F to becoming a domestic servant. For a girl of Eliza's rank to go into domestic service would have been scandalous, humiliating, and hardly likely. The job of house servant, which is held by Richardson's Pamela, was only acceptably open to women of the lower class.

24 **obliging her &:** In the original transcription, these words were followed by, "of expressing the love she bore her," a phrase Austen later crossed out. This is evidence that when JA copied her early works into the notebooks she was engaged in the process of revising phrases, rewriting sentences, and substituting words. The manuscripts of the transcriptions give us some insight into this process, but because they are fair copies, not originals, they do not reveal the writing process as well as the manuscripts of *The Watsons* or *Sanditon,* which are, as Brian Southam has observed, "heavily corrected and revised first drafts in which we are able to observe Jane Austen in the act of composition"—when, as she phrased it, she truly "lopp'd and cropp'd" (Southam, *Library*, 234).

25 **sate out:** "Sate" had a double meaning: "to sit," as used earlier, and "to set out," as the Dutchess is about to do here.

26 **about 45 & a half:** JA makes a joke of attaching the generalizing "about" to the precise age, "45 & a half." Austen uses the same device in the opening of another of her juvenile works, *Jack & Alice*: "Mr. Johnson was once upon a time about 53; in a twelve-month afterwards he was 54…" (*MW*, 12). We note with a laugh the emphasis on precise age in stories which are otherwise scant of detail.

27 **Her Emities, unconquerable:** Mr. Darcy in *Pride and Prejudice* exhibits this character flaw, and Elizabeth criticizes him for this failing. When Darcy admits his temper might be called resentful, as he "cannot forget the follies and vices of others," Elizabeth reponds, "That is a failing indeed.…Implacable resentment *is* a shade in a character" (*PP*, 58).

28 **a young Man of considerable fortune:** The idea of marrying for economic security is a recurring and often satirical theme in JA's work. Austen parodies this theme when Eliza steals a rich man from Lady Harriet and provokes the Dutchess to dispatch an army to have her tortured and put to death.

29 **seat in Surry:** "Surry" is a variant spelling of "Surrey," the county in Southeast England which is also the setting for *The Watsons* and *Emma*. The Dutchess's seat would be her main house and landholdings.

"Duke" and "duchess" were the highest ranks in the peerage of England. The duke would have a corresponding seat in the House of Lords.

30   **with the greatest Condescension:** In the eighteenth century *condescending* did not always mean *patronizing*. It could also mean consenting, assenting to an opinion, or being courteous and respectful. Sometimes JA plays on several meanings of the word.

31   **a private union:** Lord Hardwicke's Marriage Act of 1753 required a ceremony in accordance with the rites of the Anglican Church, after publication of the banns on three successive Sundays, for a valid marriage. Banns were public legal notice, made in church, proclaiming an intention of impending marriage, so that those who so desired could voice objections. A private union was illegal without a special licence, which allowed them to dispense with the banns and marry "how, where, and when they pleased" (Stone, 122).

32   **dutchess's chaplain:** Private chaplains and chapels date from the fifteenth century in England. Following the development of private pews in churches, a growing number of wealthy people all over England "secured for themselves the convenience and the status symbol of a private chaplain and therefore a private mass" (Duffy, 131). Some historians believe this privatizing tendency in religion contributed to the Reformation. Private chaplains were used as clerks, estate officers, and for some of the very rich, as doctors and astrologers as well. Private chapels and chaplains survive in England today. In *Mansfield Park*, Fanny visits a private chapel at Sotherton, dating back before James II, and observes that in bygone days prayers had been read by the "domestic chaplain." "There is," she remarks with awe, "something in a chapel and chaplain so much in character with a great house" (*MP*, vol. I, 86).

33   **to an assembly**: One of the diversions of the well-to-do in the eighteenth century was to go to public rooms called assemblies, for socializing, dancing, card playing, refreshments, and band concerts. Young girls, like Catherine Morland in *Northanger Abbey*, were taken to assemblies to meet possible suitors.

34   **300 armed men**: The Dutchess bestrides two worlds: the eighteenth-century world of assemblies and a mock medieval world. Part of the humour is giving the eighteenth-century lady the accoutrement of a duchess in a medieval legend: a private army and a personal dungeon to incarcerate her prisoners. These feudal details may have been included to appeal to Jane Austen's little brother and other boys with whom she was raised. Not only did four of her six brothers live at home during some part of her childhood, but her father tutored young boys who boarded at the Rectory, and Eliza de Feuillide's young son, Hastings, was in his mother's words, "the plaything of the whole family" (Letter to Philadelphia Walter, Oct. 26, 1792, *Austen Papers*, 150).

35   **to have them put to death in some torturelike manner:** Violence abounds in *Henry and Eliza*. The young Austen may be entertaining her juvenile audience, or responding to the violence and the wars that

dominated her era. In *Northanger Abbey*, Catherine Morland, steeped in Gothic novels, fantasizes the incarceration and even the murder of Mrs. Tilney by her "cruel" husband.

36 **Continent:** From the provincial perspective of *Henry and Eliza*, France, the nearest country, seems to constitute the continent: the words "France" and "continent" are used interchangeably.

37 **18,000 £ a year:** According to James Heldman's calculations (*Persuasions* [1990] 12: 38-49), 18,000 £ would be worth $594,000 in current U.S. currency. The average annual income for the gentry was one to ten thousand pounds a year. In *Pride and Prejudice* the women of Longbourn get excited over the riches of Bingley, a man of £5000 a year (about $165,000 in current U.S. currency).

38 **the twentieth part:** Henry and Eliza were spending twenty times more money than they actually had. Eliza de Feuillide's husband also incurred huge debts. Austen's style here is less sarcastic and obviously absurd than at other times in the novel, foreshadowing the playful and subtle humour that would characterize her later work.

39 **a man of War of 55 Guns:** By the early sixteenth century cannons were mounted on the gundecks of vessels known as men-of-war. Warships were classified acccording to the number of guns they carried: first rate—100 guns or more; second rate—84-100 guns, third rate—70-84 guns, etc. Only these three rates were used in battle (Blackburn, 365). That Eliza's ship was not up to snuff would have been amusing to JA's brother Francis, who was in the Royal Naval Academy at the time. He later fought as an admiral alongside Admiral Nelson. Charles Austen, who was to enroll in the Naval Academy at 12 years old, later also become an admiral.

40 **snug little Newgate of their Lady's:** the Dutchess's private prison. Newgate was a famous London prison dating from the twelfth century. Calling her prison a "Newgate," Austen employs the literary device of eponymy, the use of a proper name as a common noun.

41 **Her wardrobe:** The theme of money and material possessions is dominant in *Henry and Eliza* and in Austen's later novels as well. In her era people were often judged by how much money they made and consumerism was rampant. Inflation had raised the cost of necessities, but luxury items, such as gold watches, were now available to many more people.

42 **biting off two of her fingers**: In Shakespeare's *Pericles*, Cleon, alluding to the hunger in Tarsus, invokes the reverse theme of starving mothers eating their children: "Those mothers who, to nuzzle up their babes, / Thought nought too curious, are ready now / To eat those little darlings whom they loved" (*Pericles*, I, iv, 42-44).

43 **having walked 30 [miles] without stopping:** In *Pride and Prejudice* Elizabeth Bennet will walk three miles to visit Jane at Netherfield, and this is considered by Miss Bingley "to show an abominable sort of conceited independence, a most country town indifference to decorum" (*PP*, Vol. I, 32).

44 **a cold collation:** a light repast, usually consisting of light viands or delicacies (e.g., fruit, sweets, and wine) (*OED*).

45 ***Junketings***: This word is in italics in Chapman's edition to indicate that it was underlined in the manuscript, probably because it was a slang expression. According to Johnson, "junket" is a verb formed from the noun "juncate," which means a furtive or private entertainment. Johnson observes it is now improperly written "junket" in this sense "which alone remains much in use." It also means "feasting."

46 **charitable gratuity:** Eliza plans to stand outside The Red Lion Inn and beg!

47 **Postilion**: someone who rides the near horse of the leaders when two, four, or more horses are used in a carriage without a driver.

48 **you know you never even was with child:** "You was" was common usage throughout the eighteenth and nineteenth centuries, in both vulgar and aristocratic speech.

49 **breeding:** This term was in common usage to mean being pregnant. Jane Austen's mother used it in a letter of June 6, 1773 to Mrs. Walter: "My sister Cooper has made us a visit this Spring…her boy and girl are well, the youngest almost two years old, and she has not been breeding since, so perhaps she is done" (*Austen Papers*, 29). The two-year-old referred to is the Jane Cooper to whom *Henry and Eliza* is dedicated.

50 **Polly:** a nickname, usually for Mary; the abrupt shift from formality to familiarity creates the comic effect.

51 **She raised an Army**: Critics have observed that Jane Austen avoided the subject of war in her mature novels, despite the fact that she was writing in the age of political revolution. This early story was written during the time of the American Revolution and the unrest which led to the French Revolution. The spectre of war was a factor in Jane's childhood: on December 13, 1776, Mr. Austen observed a "public fast and humiliation" for the King's troops in America (Honan, 44-45).

52 **applause of her own Heart:** One of the objects of satire in this story is smugness, an exaggerated self-satisfaction. Eliza is "happy in the knowledge of her own Excellence" after stealing from her benefactors, and sings a little song about her own virtue; she responds to the Dutchess's friendship and hospitality by stealing her daughter's lover. Eliza's mother is equally smug, satisfied with the welfare of her child, and not at all guilty about having abandoned Eliza in the haycock.

Notes to *Henry and Eliza* by*:*
CATHERINE GOWL
MAGGIE HARTNICK
ANN KELLY
CASSIE MARLANTES
KAREN L. HARTNICK

AFTERWORD

In H*enry and Eliza* Jane Austen creates a character who anticipates the feminist heroines of her later novels. "Happy in the conscious knowledge of her own excellence," Eliza is confident, kind, and "sprightly." Further, she has "a noble and exalted mind." In *Pride and Prejudice*, Mr. Darcy falls in love with Elizabeth Bennet precisely "for the liveliness of [her] mind." This early Eliza, however, is also a thief and an ingrate: happening one day to steal a banknote of fifty pounds is not the act of a "noble" mind. Eliza is a character whose humanity includes weakness and taint. Austen's later heroines may be less overtly "wicked," but almost all of them have significant faults.

Austen's subsequent romance plots also recall *Henry and Eliza*. Eliza's marriage to Henry Cecil is based on "a mutual Love," but their romance does not have an easy course. Eliza must survive a series of adventures before she can marry Henry. Moreover, theirs is a marriage of inconvenience. Eliza is an outcast who was "going to Service"; Henry is promised to the Dutchess's daughter. In *Pride and Prejudice*, Elizabeth will not marry Mr. Collins even though he possesses a suitable income. She pursues love, even when that quest does not seem prudent. Both stories seem to tell us that love, pursued faithfully, can overcome all obstacles.

But the differences between this story and Austen's later works are more striking than these similarities. Most notably, Eliza is not permitted to enjoy a happy-ever-after marriage. A few paragraphs after he appears in the story, Henry dies, and Eliza is left alone to take care of her two boys and the "man of War of 55 guns" which Henry and Eliza built "in their more prosperous Days." Here and elsewhere, Austen's story is extremely unrealistic. What are we to make, for example, of Eliza's starving children "biting off two of her fingers"? Clearly, we are a long way from Box Hill! But Eliza's strength and independence reappears in more subtle and muted ways in characters such as Elinor Dashwood, Elizabeth Bennet, Emma Woodhouse, and Anne Elliot.

Eliza is not the only strong female character in *Henry and Eliza*. When the Dutchess finds that Eliza has run off with Henry, she sends her army of three hundred men to bring them back, and imprisons Eliza and her sons in her tower. Her power is all the more notable when we observe that the Duke is never mentioned in the story. When Eliza escapes from the tower and demolishes the Dutchess's castle, Austen resolves the question of her birth by blaming her problems on the misogyny of a man. "You must remember, Sir George," Eliza's new-found mother explains, "that when you sailed for America, you left me breeding...dreading your just resentment at her not proving the Boy you wished, I took her to a Haycock and laid her down."

Perhaps the strongest of Jane Austen's feminist convictions is her belief in the importance of self-gratification. Eliza is reconciled with her parents, wins back her fortune, and levels the Dutchess's Newgate. She wins "the blessings of thousands," but in the story's concluding sentence, Austen emphasizes that she has also earned "the Applause of her own Heart." Eliza understands the necessity of a sense of self-worth, and like Austen's other heroines, she is as proud as she is intelligent. But Austen also suggests that Eliza awards herself more applause than she merits.

Insofar as *Henry and Eliza* has a moral, it is not that good things come to those who wait or to those who are unequivocally good. Eliza is a strong, assertive, and at times slightly wicked character. In her later novels, Austen invents more realistic heroines who stand somewhere between Eliza and the perfect lady. But in these figures we can still recognize the self-inventing energy that is so appealing in Eliza.

ANN KELLY

WORKS CITED AND CONSULTED

Austen, Jane. *The Works of Jane Austen*: Volume VI: *Minor Works*, ed. R.W. Chapman, as revised by B.C. Southam. Oxford:Oxford University Press, 1987.

―――――. *Jane Austen's Letters*, ed. Deirdre Le Faye. Oxford: Oxford University Press, 1995.

―――――. *The Works of Jane Austen*, vols. I-V, ed. R.W. Chapman. Oxford:Oxford University Press, 3rd edition, 1965-67.

―――――. *Volume the First*, ed. R.W. Chapman. London: TheAthlone Press, 1984. (Reprinted from the Clarendon Press edition, 1925.)

Austen-Leigh, W. and R.A., revised and enlarged by Deirdre Le Faye. *Jane Austen: A Family Record*. London: Smith Elly, 1993.

Austen-Leigh, R.A. *Jane Austen. Her Life and Letters, A Family Record*. London: Smith Elly, 1913.

―――――. *Austen Papers 1704-1856*. London: Spottiswoode, Ballantyne & Co., Ltd., 1942.

Blackburn, Graham. *The Illustrated Encyclopedia of Ships, Boats, Vessels and other Water-borne Crafts*. Woodstock: The Outlook Press, 1978.

Bradbrook, Frank W. *Jane Austen and Her Predecessors*. Cambridge: Cambridge University Press, 1967.

Brown, Julia Prewitt. *A Reader's Guide to the Nineteenth-Century English Novel*. New York: Macmillan Publishing Company, 1985.

Butler, Marilyn. *Jane Austen and the War of Ideas*. Oxford: Clarendon Press, 1975.

Chapman, R.W. *Jane Austen: Facts and Problems*. Oxford: Oxford University Press, 1948.

Chapone, Hester. *The Works of Mrs. Chapone*. Boston: W. Wells and T.B. Wait & Co., 1809.

Doody, Margaret Anne and Douglas Murray, eds. *Jane Austen: Catharine and Other Writings*. Oxford: Oxford University Press, 1993.

Duffy, Eamon. *The Stripping of the Altars: Traditional Religion in England c.1400-c.1580*. New Haven & London: Yale University Press, 1992.

Fergus, Jan. *Jane Austen: A Literary Life*. London: The Macmillan Press, Ltd., 1991.

Fordyce, James, D.D. *Sermons to Young Women*. Volumes I and II. London: Printed for A. Miller and T. Cadell in The Strand, 1766.

Grey, J. David, ed. *The Jane Austen Companion*. New York: Macmillan, 1986.

—————. *The Jane Austen Handbook*. London: The Athlone Press, 1986.

—————. *Jane Austen's Beginnings: The Juvenilia and Lady Susan*. Ann Arbor and London: UMI Research Press, 1989.

Heldman, James. "How Wealthy is Darcy——Really?" *Persuasions* 12, December 16, 1990, 38-49.

Honan, Park. *Jane Austen: Her Life*. London: Weidenfeld & Nicolson, 1987.

Johnson, Samuel. *A Dictionary of the English Language*. (2 volumes) London: W Stradan for J. & P. Knapton, 1755-56 (Second edition).

Lascelles, Mary. *Jane Austen and Her Art*. Oxford: Oxford University Press, 1939.

Lennox, Charlotte. *The Female Quixote, or The Adventures of Arabella*. Oxford: Oxford University Press, 1989.

Litz, A. Walton. *Jane Austen: A Study of Her Artistic Development*. New York: Oxford University Press, 1965.

Opie, Iona, ed. *The Oxford Book of Nursery Rhymes*. Oxford: Clarendon Press, 1989.

Oxford English Dictionary (second edition) Oxford: Clarendon Press, 1989.

Richmond, Colin. "Religion and the Fifteenth-Century English Gentleman," *The Church, Politics and Patronage in the Fifteenth Century*, ed. Barrie Dobson. New York: St. Martin's Press, 1984.

Southam, Brian C. "The Juvenilia," in *The Works of Jane Austen*, Volume VI, *Minor Works*, ed. R.W. Chapman. Oxford: Oxford University Press, 1982.

—————, ed. *Critical Essays on Jane Austen*. London: Routledge & K. Paul, 1968.

—————. "The Manuscript of Jane Austen's *Volume the First*," *The Library* (Transactions of the Bibliographical Society). Fifth Series, Vol XVII, No. 3 (September 1962), 231-237.

—————. *Jane Austen's Literary Manuscripts*. Oxford: Oxford University Press, 1964.

—————, ed. *Jane Austen's 'Sir Charles Grandison'*. Oxford: The Clarendon Press, 1980.

The Spectator. Volume VIII. London: printed by T. Beasley, 1797.

Stone, Laurence. *Road to Divorce*. Oxford: Oxford University Press, 1990.

Tompkins, J.M.S. *The Popular Novel in England 1770-1800*. Lincoln: University of Nebraska Press, 1961.

Woolf, Virginia. *The Common Reader*. New York: Harcourt Brace & Co., 1948.

The Juvenilia Press is an enterprise that combines scholarship with pedagogy. It is designed to publish editions of early works of known writers, in a simple format, with student involvement. Each volume, besides the text by the young author (of any age up to 20), includes light-hearted illustration, scholarly annotation, and an introduction that relates this work to the author's mature writing. It thus provides an opportunity for scholars and apprentice scholars to practise editing the apprentice work of their authors.

Available volumes are priced between $4 and $7.

VOLUMES IN THE SERIES:

GENERAL EDITOR: Juliet McMaster